Write a Poem Step by Step

A Simple, Logical Plan You Can Follow to Create Your Own Poems

JoAnn Early Macken

Published by Earlybird Press, September 2012
First Edition

ISBN-10: 0985765003
ISBN-13: 978-0-9857650-0-2

Cover design: Tammy West, tammy@westgraphix.com
Earlybird Press logo: Billy Macken, wmacken@wisc.edu

For Gene

www.joannmacken.com

Contents

Introduction

When I first wanted to write poetry for children, I found plenty of wonderful poems to read, but I didn't know how to begin on my own. So I studied books of poetry, books about writing, and books about writing poetry. I compiled a list of what I thought were the most important components, or ingredients, of a good poem. I put my list into a logical order by thinking about what came first and then what built on that. I turned my list of poetry ingredients into a method of writing a poem. Each item from my list became a step, or part of a step, in the process.

As a student in the Master of Fine Arts in Writing for Children and Young Adults Program at Vermont College of Fine Arts, I described those important ingredients in my critical thesis, "What Makes a Poem a Poem?" I gave a graduating lecture called "Yes, You Can! Write Your Own Poem." I started sharing my method with students of all ages.

I received the Barbara Juster Esbensen 2000 Poetry Teaching Award for my work with a class of third graders who all wrote amazing poems. (Some of them appear in this book.) I've used the same logical method to help thousands of students write their own poems in poetry writing workshops. I've shared the method with teachers at Wisconsin State Reading Association and International Reading Association conventions. I've received valuable input from students and teachers, and as I've learned which techniques work best, I've reorganized, refined, and fine-tuned the method.

This book begins with the first step—finding a good idea—and walks you through the process all the way to a polished draft. You'll find tips, suggestions, and examples written by students in my poetry writing workshops. Now you can follow the process step by step and write your own poems, too!

How to Use this Book

The how-to-write portion of this book is divided into five steps:

Step 1. Finding Ideas
Step 2. Using Imagery
Step 3. Using Exciting Language
Step 4. Creating Patterns
Step 5. Creating the Form

By following these chapters in order, you can write a draft of a new poem, one step at a time. If you've never written a poem before, you can use this process to begin writing poetry. If you already have a method that works for you, you might find that this approach makes the process a little smoother. You might also discover techniques that you haven't tried before. You'll find at least one example for each step. All the poems, except for a few I wrote myself, were written by students in my poetry workshops.

The first step helps you find an idea to write about. If you already have an idea, the "Finding Ideas" chapter will help you decide whether it's a good one—one that is likely to work through the rest of the process and result in a solid draft of a new poem.

Each of the remaining steps builds on your earlier work. You can go back to a previous step (or the one before that) at any time. If you feel your poem is not working for any reason, you can set it aside and try another one.

Follow all five steps in order at least once. Until you're familiar with the whole process, you'll get the best results by working through it step by step. You might find that this method works for you just as it is, or it might lead you to discover a method that works even better for you.

The chapter following Step 5, "Forms," describes specific forms of poems that you might enjoy writing. They include free verse, haiku, limericks, odes, list poems, and shape poems. You'll also find titles of poetry collections that demonstrate these and other forms, as well as other poetry writing books you can turn to for tips and encouragement. The more you read, the better you'll understand what makes a poem a poem. You'll find poets whose work you enjoy and want to keep reading. You might also find inspiration for more poems!

The next chapter, "Writing Exercises," gives you some ideas for ways to get more creative.

After you finish a poem, you can revise it right away. Or you can set it aside for a time while you take a break or work on another poem. You'll find tips for revising in the next chapter, "Revising."

Finally, in "Publishing Your Work," you'll find information about sharing the poems you've written.

Keep in mind that a poem cannot be written according to a formula. Although this book describes some of the key ingredients of poetry, it's not a recipe to be followed precisely. It's more like a travel guide that encourages you to venture off in your own direction. Not every poem includes every technique mentioned here. Each poem, like each poet, is unique.

Poets and scholars have debated for centuries about the importance of various aspects of poetry. This book explains my thoughts, which are based on my own reading, work with students and teachers, and process of discovery. That process continues: I'm still learning, still reading, still fine-tuning the method. Part of the joy of reading and writing poetry is that you can decide for yourself what makes a poem a poem. This book gives you the tools to make a more informed decision. See what you think!

Getting Ready to Write

The best way to become comfortable with poetry is to read as much of it as you can. By reading, you begin to recognize how poems work. The more familiar you are with the tools of poetry, the easier and more fun it is for you to create your own poems. Learning by reading also enables you to build on what has already been done, to take it a step further. Be sure to explore the suggested titles throughout this book and on my web site, www.joannmacken.com.

If you make writing a pleasure, you are more likely to keep at it. Writing poetry takes practice, so make it easy to keep going. Give yourself plenty of time and space to learn how you work comfortably. Try different settings, different times of day, and different kinds of paper and writing instruments.

Do you have a favorite place to work, or do you enjoy trying out different locations? You might want to sit at a desk or a table in a quiet library. You might like to curl up in a big, soft chair or even in your bed. Depending on the weather, you might enjoy being outside in your yard, in a park, or at the beach. Find a comfortable spot where you won't be interrupted.

Do you have a favorite kind of pen, pencil, or paper? Do you write longhand or type at a computer or word processor? Experiment to find out what works best for you. I'm inspired by purple ink. I write my first drafts by hand in spiral notebooks or on legal pads or loose leaf paper.

Does listening to music invigorate you, inspire you, or distract you? Certain kinds of music help some people focus. I prefer quiet. See what works for you.

Don't worry about spelling, punctuation, or penmanship until you're ready to show your work to someone else. First drafts can be as messy as they need to be, as long as you can make sense of what they say so you can revise them into later drafts.

Once I have a first draft on paper, I revise until I'm satisfied, writing copy after copy by hand so I can try different variations. Next, I type a draft on the computer. I print that draft, scribble all over it, and keep working until I think I'm finished. Then I share my work with a group of writers I trust to give me their honest impressions.

Whenever you think of an idea or even a word that grabs you, jot it down on paper so you won't forget it. If you carry a notebook and pen around with you and use them, you won't lose track of the tantalizing ideas that pop into your mind at odd moments. You'll have a list of topics ready for the next time you feel the urge to write. Over time, you might see ideas repeated or patterns evolving. Then you'll know there is a subject you care about just waiting to be explored. Pay attention to those subjects—they could result in your most interesting work!

Voice

No two people are exactly alike. Each person has a unique point of view because we all come from different backgrounds and have different kinds of experiences. Even if one hundred people wrote a poem about the same topic, each poem would be different because we all see things in different ways.

Because no one else sees things quite the way you do, no one else can write exactly like you do. The words you choose and the way you arrange them are uniquely your own. They express your voice.

Voice is what makes your poem sound exactly like yours and no one else's. Your ideas and the words you use to describe them come from your own experience. Your voice comes both from being yourself and from making a conscious effort to express your thoughts in new ways. A writer's voice develops gradually over time and with practice, so be patient.

Show the world the true you when you write your poems. Stretch to find the very best words and arrangements. Play with patterns. Experiment with different line breaks and forms. Have fun with the process—you'll learn something new from each experiment you try!

Step 1. Finding Ideas

I believe a poem should express an idea. Whether it's serious or silly, formal or informal, it should have something to say to a reader. A poem should make a connection, make an impression, make a point. It doesn't have to be profound or moving. It just has to say what you mean.

A poem doesn't need a plot like a story does. Nothing has to happen. It can be just a quick observation or glimpse—like a snapshot of something you notice. But it should say something to a reader, even if it's as simple as, "Hey, look what I found!"

The first step in writing a poem is to decide what to write about. Ideas are all around you. All you have to do is open yourself up to them. The best way to discover an idea of your own is to slow down and pay attention. Take a good look at the everyday things around you. You'll find some that are truly amazing! Have you ever looked closely at a spider web? Do you notice the moon and stars shining on a clear night? Do you enjoy the sound of rain when you are snug and warm inside? Does the taste of a tart apple bring back a vivid memory? When you slow down and pay attention, you'll find ideas everywhere.

Spend time thinking about your ideas. As you walk around, pay attention. Look closely at what you see. Listen to the sounds that surround you. Smell the aromas. Feel the textures of objects you find and notice the differences between them. Use all your senses.

Let yourself daydream. Imagine. Ponder. Look out the window. Stare up at the ceiling. Close your eyes and listen. What do you hear? Anything you can experience with any of your senses can become part of a poem. So can anything you make up.

Some people believe they need an idea before they can start to write. I've found that the opposite is often true. Putting a pen to paper and beginning to write sometimes starts ideas flowing. Try it! You might want to begin by spilling out whatever is on your mind onto paper to clear some space for new ideas.

A story can explore a whole string of ideas. A poem needs only one. This chapter will help you pick a good one.

What Makes an Idea a Good Idea?

If a teacher assigns you a topic to write about, you might have to struggle to come up with your own approach to the subject. That struggle adds pressure. It makes writing a poem more like work than fun. To be creative, you need to relax and let go, not worry about finding something to say. If you choose your own topic, you can choose one you want to write about. Here are some tips to help you choose a topic that will hold your interest for as long as it takes to write a draft of a poem.

Write About Something You Care About

My first tip about choosing an idea applies to almost any kind of writing: Write about something you care about. How can you put your heart into a subject that doesn't move you? If you try to write about something you don't care about, you might have to force yourself to find something to say. You might struggle to write anything interesting at all. Your poem could suffer. It might even be boring. So write about something you feel strongly about.

That doesn't necessarily mean something you like! Something that makes you feel an emotion, whether happy or sad, curious or angry, silly or serious, can make a good topic for a poem. Anything can be a subject if you are open to it: your shoes, the chair you're sitting on, what you ate for breakfast—as long as you care about it.

Chloe's poem shows how much piano music means to her and why.

The Piano

The piano reminds me of my grandma
When she played the beautiful sounds

The piano smells like an old library
When you step in and smell the old, dusty books

The piano makes me feel like I'm flying
Through white, fluffy clouds in the sky

The piano sounds like twinkling stars
The beautiful sounds are no louder than a soft MEOW from my cat

Chloe Strait, Grade 5

Put your whole heart into your poem. Go ahead and reveal your emotions. The effort will show in your writing.

Write About Familiar Things

The better you know something, the easier it is to write about. Focus on something you understand or are eager to investigate. If you don't know your subject well enough, you might struggle to say anything about it. You can use your imagination to write about something unfamiliar, but be sure you can see, hear, smell, feel, and/or taste your subject in your mind.

Try to see familiar things in a new way. A poem can be about an everyday thing like a spoon, a toothbrush, or even a pencil.

The Pencil

The pencil is as sharp as a needle and as light as a feather
And as I write it gets smaller and smaller and smaller like a shrinking man
until I can't write anymore.

James Marquardt III, Grade 5

Be Specific

Remember that a poem needs only one idea. Pick out one topic, one object, or one event, and focus on that. Write about one tree, one star, one flower, or one person. If you try to write about a topic as broad as "dogs," for example, you might have trouble finding anything to say that holds true for all dogs. Most dogs bark and have four legs and a tail. But not all of them do. Dogs come in so many different varieties and sizes and shapes and colors and textures and sounds that you might find it impossible to say anything accurate. The subject is too broad. But if you narrow it down and write about one specific dog—especially a dog you also know and care about—you can write about its size, shape, color, smell, name, bark, actions, personality, and so on.

Matt's poem describes one specific thing: lightning.

Lightning

Flash!
Lightning shoots through the sky
it is as sharp as a needle
and is taller than the tallest skyscraper
it is as painful as falling off a giant tree
a tiny bolt of lightning can destroy things
and it can make the electricity go out
Flash!

Matt Mann, Grade 4

Brainstorming

The goal of this first step is to find a good idea to write about. In Step 2, you'll begin to write your own poem based on that idea. First, remember the three main requirements for a good idea:

- something you care about
- something familiar
- something specific

The next few pages include questions to help you come up with ideas for your own poems. The example poems show you some approaches other students have tried. One of them might give you an idea for a topic of your own.

As you read the questions and poems, jot down any ideas that pop into your mind. You might find several ideas you can keep in a list. You need only one good idea to go on to Step 2, but having an extra one or two tucked away for later gives you the option of making a fresh start if you get stuck. You can also refer back to your list any time you want to write another poem.

Now for the questions:

What do you care about? This is a broad question that can have many good answers. Think about people, places, and things.

Is there a friend or family member you'd like to write about? Who would you like to say something to? What would you say?

Could you write about your classroom, your home, or wherever you are right now? Look around you. What do you notice? Is there a special spot you like to visit? Have you taken a trip or a vacation? Gone on an adventure?

What is your favorite food? How about your least favorite? Olivia uses all her senses to give us her impression of spinach.

Spinach

Green like grass and white like a cloud,
Wet like rain, smooth like silk and
Crunchy like a cracker,
Quiet like a table but crunchy like a cracker,
An unripe tomato mixed with stale lettuce,
Yucky, mucky, smelly, ugly, rainy, gloomy,
Yuck.

Olivia Poole, Grade 2

Do you have a pet? Your dog, cat, turtle, horse, iguana, duck, or gerbil could be a good subject for a poem.

Do you like to listen to music? Do you play a musical instrument?

Do you have a favorite time of year? What kind of weather do you enjoy? What kind would you rather avoid?

Do you have a favorite holiday? What kinds of traditions does your family practice? Could you write about a celebration?

What else do you know about? A hobby? An animal, an insect, a bird, or a plant?

Arthur knows about owls.

The Owl

The owl has one ear higher
One ear lower
Eyes as big as light bulbs
He is as silent as a spy.

Arthur Bleksley, Grade 3

What do you think about? Is something often on your mind? Does one subject or question keep coming back to you?

Do you ever remember your dreams? Pleasant, funny, confusing, or frightening, dreams can be rich sources of ideas.

What do you wonder about? If you think about something a lot (outer space, the future, or how something works, for example), you might come up with your own creative explanations. How does a caterpillar turn into a butterfly? What does a crow think? What makes a flower bloom or a chipmunk hibernate or a tall tree grow from a tiny seed? Anything you've ever wondered about can be a good topic for a poem.

Erin wonders about a star.

A Star

I look at a star.
Is it near or is it far?
Does it play hopscotch or jump rope?
Does it have friends or a teacher?
Does it eat muffins or mac and cheese?
I don't know. I will never know.
That's good so I can keep wondering.

Erin Szablewski, Grade 4

Slow down and take a careful look around. You can find ideas everywhere. Write down any that you might like to write a poem about. Can you see something right now that interests you? If you do, put it on your list.

Miguel writes about his imagination.

My Imagination

My mind plays tricks on me
in the dark.
An invisible man
in my closet
is wearing my jacket and shoes.

Miguel Rowell-Ortiz, Grade 3

Do you have a few ideas? Before you go on to Step 2, choose one.

Pick an idea that is specific, that you know about, and that you care about right now. Then you'll be ready to begin writing your poem. You can always use the other ideas later, and you can add more ideas to your list whenever something grabs your attention.

Step 2. Using Imagery

In this step, you begin to write a poem about one of your ideas. You start by listing imagery inspired by the idea you chose. At the end of this step, you'll have a list that will become a poem as you work through the rest of the steps.

When you think of imagery, think of an image or a picture. First, let's start with an exercise. Close your eyes for a moment and think of your home.

What came into your mind when you closed your eyes? An apartment building or a cottage? Your bedroom? The kitchen? A person in your family? A pet?

Did you see any words? Probably not. Most people think in pictures.

Yes, most people think in pictures. Our task as writers and poets is to put the pictures, or images, we see in our minds into words so that other people can see what we see. But imagery is not only about what we see. It also includes "pictures" from our other senses. We can use imagery to help others hear what we hear, taste what we taste, smell what we smell, feel what we feel, and imagine what we imagine. We can use all our senses to create vivid descriptions.

One way to give someone else a picture is to compare it to something else. Comparing something new to something familiar is one way to help others understand it. A comparison can be obvious, or it can be surprising.

You've probably heard phrases such as "light as a feather," or "slept like a log." These are examples of one type of comparison called a *simile*. A simile uses the words *like* or *as*.

Kelly's poem is a sad one about saying goodbye to her cat. Notice all the similes she uses to describe her feelings.

Bye Bye

I feel as sad as a hound
as slow as a turtle
as hard as rocks
as mad as a lion
as long as a river
as hot as lava
as sleepy as a person home from work
as small as an ant.
My cat is in heaven.

Kelly Sween, Grade 3

In Kelly's poem, each line but the last one compares how she feels using *as*. Look for the words *like* and *as* to find a simile.

Another type of comparison, a *metaphor*, does not use the words like or as but says that something is something else. A metaphor you might have heard before is "Time is money." Literally, of course, time is not money, but the metaphor points out that they have something important in common. Look for a metaphor in the first line of Athena's poem.

Black Leader

On his face two amber jewels shine
Alert and soulful
Fur as dark as the shadows,
a spirit as lively as the wind
Pink tongue lolled out
Sharp pearls glimmer in his mouth
Never knowing of fear,
his tail raised like a majestic flag
A hunter of stealth,
leader of the chase
His chest deep with pride
Father of mischievous pups
Erect ears twitching curiously

No rustle
No bark
Slowly, he forms his mouth to a perfect "o"
From his body comes a mysterious song,
hovering in the air and subsiding in pitch
Silence
An eerie answer echoes through the wooded valley,
and he turns,
his sleek body bounding off
His legs carrying him like a rushing river
The black alpha
The leader

Athena Naylor, Grade 6

In this poem, the line "On his face two amber jewels shine" compares the wolf's eyes to jewels without using *like* or *as*. That comparison is a metaphor. Another metaphor is in the line "Sharp pearls glimmer in his mouth," which compares his teeth to pearls.

Personification is another way to give a reader a picture. It means giving human qualities to something that isn't human or describing something that is not alive as if it is alive.

Jimmy describes how a daisy behaves.

Blooming

The daisy opens like a book.
The leaves do stretching exercises
warming up in the sun.

Jimmy Macken, Grade 3

Of course, a plant doesn't exercise like a person does. "The leaves do stretching exercises / warming up in the sun" is an example of personification.

Symbolism uses an image to stand for something else. A stop sign is a symbol: people know the meaning of the shape and color even if they can't read the word. A flag is a symbol that stands for a country. A dark night might symbolize mystery or danger. In the next poem, look for a symbol in the last line.

Traveling by Foot

My feet feel harsh
as if someone stepped on my toe.
It's taking so long
it feels as if
the mountain reaches the sky.
I feel like a person that doesn't have a compass.
I feel like I've lost my wisdom.
My head is like a bear's head
when he's irritated from people bothering him.
I see what you see
when you're a cartoon
and there's stars above your head.

Sam Gilbertson, Grade 2

If you've ever watched cartoons, you probably recognize that a character with stars above his head is confused. The stars are a symbol of confusion.

Using imagery, including similes, metaphors, personification, and symbols, can add depth, richness, and meaning to your poetry.

Clustering

One helpful method to come up with images that fit your subject is called clustering. Start by writing your topic in the middle of a page and drawing a circle around it. Then write words that relate to your subject around the circle. Draw a circle around each related word and connect it to the central circle with a line. Give yourself a time limit. Ten minutes might be long enough.

I decided to write about a stone I found on the beach, so I started clustering with the word *stone*. Then I added words the stone made me think of—the words you see here—and connected them.

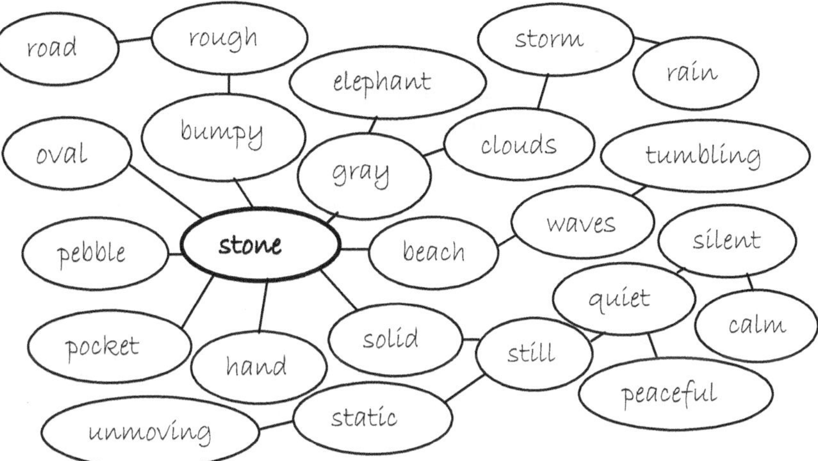

A cluster can end up in almost any shape. This cluster branched out more to one side than the other as I followed and connected my thoughts. Three images came to my mind as I looked at it:

gray as an elephant
gray as a storm cloud
rough as a bumpy road

Besides the images, other words and phrases came to me, too. You'll read more about them and the poem that resulted from this cluster in the chapters that follow.

Writing Time

What kinds of imagery might fit your idea? Try to use all your senses plus your imagination and your feelings when you think about your subject. Try clustering with the topic of your poem. You might come up with some original images that surprise you.

In your new list, write all the imagery you can think of: similes, metaphors, symbols, and personification. Use specific words that paint a clear picture for your readers. Don't just describe your topic—go a step further and compare it to something else. This list is the start of your poem.

You can write about any characteristic you can detect with any of your senses. Remember to compare your subject to something else; don't just describe it. Stretch your mind! Don't settle for something obvious. The most surprising comparisons can be the most interesting. Write down everything that comes to mind even if at first you don't see a logical connection. The sense of the concept might come to you later.

For example, a new bike might be as brown and shiny as a June bug. A hopping frog could bounce like a ball. Try not to use a comparison you've heard before, such as "white as snow," "blue as the sky," or "green like grass." Take time to think of a new way to describe your subject.

Here are some questions to help you think of comparisons. You don't have to answer all of them, just the ones that make sense to you for the topic you're working on. If you have an answer, or if a question gives you an idea for another image, put it on your list.

What can you compare your subject to? What does it look like? What does it remind you of? Think about its actions, its speed, and any other characteristics such as these:

shape: as round as a cookie, square like a window
patterns: striped like a tiger
color: yellow like a sunflower
size: as tiny as a ladybug, as wide as a street
temperature: as hot as sand on a sunny beach
movement: inching along like a caterpillar

Does your subject make any noise? What else makes that kind of sound? A frog? A jet? A popcorn popper? How loud is it? As loud as a siren? As quiet as a cricket?

What does it feel like? Smooth like a table or rough like a carpet?

Does it have a smell? What does it smell like? Lilies of the valley? A wet dog? A swimming pool?

If your subject is something you can taste, what does it taste like? Sour like lemons or sweet like a cherry? What kind of texture does it have? Slippery like ice cream or crunchy like a nut?

What does your subject's name mean to you? What kind of personality does it have? What kind of mood is it in? What does it want? Where did it come from, and where is it going?

You might want to speak to your subject. What would you say?

How would you feel if you were the subject you are writing about? You can also write from your subject's point of view.

When you've written every image you can think of, you'll be ready for Step 3. Before you go on, take a look at the images in your list. Do they work together? Do they reinforce each other? If not, don't feel that you have to use them all. Choose your best lines. It might help to circle them or copy them over so that you can see them together. Don't worry about wasting any extras. You can always use them in another poem.

The cluster example in this chapter gave me three images. Two of them seemed to fit best with the topic of the stone I was describing: "gray as a storm cloud" and "rough as a bumpy road." I kept those two images in my poem-starter list. The image of an elephant didn't fit with the others, so I saved it for another poem.

In the next three steps, you'll add exciting words to your list of images, reorganize your list with patterns, and shape it to make it look like a poem. Remember that if your first idea doesn't work out, you can begin again with another topic at any time.

Step 3. Using Exciting Language

Poetry focuses on language. The vocabulary of poetry includes exciting words, not just ordinary, everyday ones. When you put an image from your mind into words others can understand, try to create the clearest possible picture. To do that, use the best possible words to convey that image. Then readers can see what you see, hear what you hear, feel what you feel, and so on.

Some poets use words that readers might not recognize. Why would a poet use a more complicated, less familiar word? Maybe to capture the reader's imagination. If you are not sure of the meaning of a word, look it up in a dictionary. You might find helpful information about the origin of the word or additional meanings you weren't aware of.

To find exactly the right word, you can also check a thesaurus. There you'll find an assortment of words with similar meanings so you can choose exactly the right one.

Here are some types of exciting words.

Specific Words

To get a picture or an idea across clearly, use specific words rather than general ones. If you mention a tree, say whether it is an oak, an elm, or a maple. If you write about a dog, call it a Dalmatian, a beagle, a poodle, or whatever. To give an accurate picture of the bird you see, describe it as a cardinal, a robin, a blue jay, and so on.

Instead of telling how you feel, show your reactions. If you are excited or nervous or scared about something, describe how you behave. Do you jump up and down and shout? Nibble your fingernails? Hide behind your hair? Those details show your emotions in a more interesting, personal way than a plain statement of how you feel.

Words like *nice*, *pretty*, *beautiful*, and *lovely* give readers an impression of your feelings about the subject, but not a clear picture. Instead, give your readers a better understanding by using your senses to describe it.

In her poem, Ariella uses specific language to describe shadows.

Shadows

Shadows loom behind you like a
Silent spy,
As quiet as a motionless feather.
In the dark they disappear but
Come again in the day.

Ariella Cobb, Grade 3

Specific words such as *loom*, *silent*, and *motionless* add interest to a poem and give readers a clear picture.

Active Words

The difference between "The cake was baked" and "I baked a cake" is the difference between passive and active language. One problem with the first sentence is that it doesn't say who baked the cake. The second sentence is clearer because it supplies the missing information.

Look for any form of the verb *to be*, such as *is*, *are*, *was*, *were*, *am*, *be*, *being*, and *been*. Try to substitute a more active verb. For example, you could change "The bird was flying" to "The bird flew."

Instead of ordinary, everyday verbs like *went* or *walked*, try to use more exciting words, such as *galloped*, *skedaddled*, or *slithered*. See the next poem for examples.

The Storm

The storm is as strong
as a wild horse.
It stomps on a tree.
Thud!
the leaves flutter
like hummingbirds.

Chris Tonellato, Grade 3

Notice the active verbs *stomps* and *flutter* in Chris's poem. They make the poem come alive!

Words that Fit the Subject

Tempo means rate of speed. A poem can be quick and lively, slow and soothing, or angry and stomping. The words you choose affect the tempo of each line.

Use words that fit the subject of your poem. For example, in a poem about a hippopotamus, use words that sound large and heavy, such as *lumber* or *wallow*. In a poem about a sparrow, look for words that sound small and light, such as *flit* or *twitter*. In this poem about a mouse, look for words that make you think of a mouse.

Mouse

Cheese nibbler,
Hole maker,
Can knocker,
Gray
As blurry as comets,
A scurrying, squeaky shadow
Following me
To darkness

Marah Sutherland, Grade 3

Did you notice *nibbler*, *scurrying*, and *squeaky*? Such words sound like mouse words and fit the subject of the poem. Can you think of some soft, squirmy words you could use to describe a worm? How about whooshing words to describe the wind?

Words with Interesting Sounds

The sounds of words contribute to their meaning. Some words sound harsh. Others sound soft. Some words feel quiet, and others feel loud. If you have a choice of two or more words with similar meanings to use in your poem, use the one that sounds best.

Remember the clustering exercise from Step 2? I liked the way the words *oval* and *pebble* sounded together, so I put them on my list to use in my poem. Other exciting words from that exercise appealed to me, too: *still*, *tumbling*, and *pocket*. I added them all to my list.

Alliteration

Which sounds more interesting, "active noisy honeybee" or "busy buzzing bumblebee"? In the second example, the repetition of the *b* sounds is pleasing to hear. Alliteration is the repetition of the sound at the beginning of several words in a series. Two more examples of alliteration are "slithery, slippery snakes" and "wet, wild, windy weather."

Many tongue twisters use alliteration. Here are some examples:

> She sells seashells by the seashore.
> Peter Piper picked a peck of pickled peppers.
> How much wood would a woodchuck chuck if a woodchuck could chuck wood?

In many cases, alliteration is what makes tongue twisters hard to say. It also makes them fun. A poem with a lot of alliteration can sound humorous. If you are writing a serious poem, use alliteration sparingly.

The Tiger

The stripes of a tiger are just like grass
Hungry, hunting, harmful
Sounds of its roar can be heard far away
Hungry, hunting, harmful
Faster than a car
Silent as a tree
Hungry, hunting, harmful
As fast as a second in time
There for only a small eye blink
Hungry, hunting, harmful

Raul Salgado, Grade 3

In Raul's poem, "Hungry, hunting, harmful" is alliteration.

Onomatopoeia

Words that sound like what they describe add life as well as meaning to your poem. Think of them as sound effects. Some examples are *boom*, *crash*, *rustle*, *chirp*, *hiccup*, and *tweet*. Can you think of any others? What is the sound of a raindrop landing in a puddle? What do you hear when you walk through a pile of dry leaves in fall? What kind of a noise does a doorbell make?

Thunderstorm

Wet.
A big flash of light and a BOOM!
Drip drop drip drop.
Dark.

Melanie Gilmore, Grade 3

Onomatopoeia makes Melanie's poem fun to read aloud. Try saying "BOOM!" loudly and "Drip drop drip drop" quietly.

Invented Words

Some poets make up words when no existing word will do. Use this technique sparingly—and only when a reader can understand the meaning from the context.

The Beach

The waves come
and crash on shore.
Shosh, shwash, shosh, shwash
The sand is as smooth as a wooden polished floor.
The sand goes through my toes.
The day was as hot as a heating vent.
I built a sandcastle,
but the waves washed it away.
Shosh, shwash, shosh, shwash.

Sarah Ilbek, Grade 3

The line "Shosh, shwash, shosh, shwash" includes invented words that sound like waves crashing on the beach.

Writing Time

Now go back to the list you made of imagery that describes your idea. First look for ordinary words in your list. Substitute exciting words wherever you can. Remember the kinds of language discussed in this chapter:

- specific words
- active words
- words that fit the subject
- words with interesting sounds
- alliteration
- onomatopoeia
- invented words

Try to think of these kinds of words that fit your topic.

Are some of your lines single exciting words? Look for ways to combine them into interesting lines. My list included *oval*, *pebble*, *still*, *tumbling*, and *pocket*. From those five words, I added these three lines to my two images:

> tumbled by waves
> I hold this oval pebble in my pocket
> and remember stillness

Notice that I did not use the exact form of each word: *tumbling* became *tumbled*, and *still* became *stillness*. Feel free to play with words until the form and tense feel right.

Add to your list any additional exciting words and phrases that fit your topic. Close your eyes and picture the subject. What else comes to mind? Keep adding exciting words that describe your subject. Write everything down. Even if you don't use a word in this draft, you might decide later to put it back in. Or it might fit better in another poem.

Again, before you go on to the next step, choose your best lines. Mark them or copy them over so you can see them together. Remember that you don't have to use everything in your list. Some lines might not fit with others. You might even have enough material for more than one poem.

Put the lines you want to keep into an order that makes sense to you. Do you see a logical time sequence? Do the words in some lines sound better in a certain order? Do the lines build to reinforce a certain feeling?

Your list is becoming a poem. You will see it happen as you continue through the next two steps. Next, you will work on creating patterns in your poem. Finally, you will give it a form by dividing the lines.

Step 4. Creating Patterns

In this step, you expand and reorganize your poem-in-progress, keeping patterns in mind. Three patterns are important in poetry: rhythm, rhyme, and repetition.

Rhythm

Rhythm is the regular pattern of sound in language. It's like the beat in music. Many people think rhythm is the main difference between poetry and prose.

The rhythm of a poem should match its feeling or mood: slow and smooth for a serious topic, quicker for a fun one. "He bounced up and down like a ping pong ball" has a rhythm that sounds like bouncing. Choose words that help you achieve that kind of fit. To hear its rhythm, read a poem aloud.

Meter

When you listen to some poems read aloud, you can tap or clap along with their rhythm. Your taps or claps most likely mark the syllables that are heavily stressed when they are spoken: MAry HAD a LITtle LAMB.

Heavily and lightly stressed syllables give a poem its rhythm. In some poems, the heavily and lightly stressed syllables form a regular pattern. To meter means to measure, and poems with regular rhythm patterns are called metered or metric.

Metrical Feet

Each line of a poem can be divided into sections called feet. Each foot has one heavily stressed syllable, so you can count the heavily stressed syllables to know the number of feet in a line.

Different types of feet include different patterns of heavily and lightly stressed syllables. You don't have to memorize their names, but understanding their differences can help you keep your rhythm consistent. Here are some common types of feet.

The most familiar type of foot is the *iamb*, which has two syllables. The first syllable is lightly stressed, and the second one is heavily stressed. The rhythm of an iamb sounds like "da DUM." Here are some words that fit this pattern:

escape (es CAPE)
raccoon (rac COON)
enjoy (en JOY)

Another common type of foot with two syllables is the *trochee*, which has the stronger stress on the first syllable. Here are some one-word examples:

insect (IN sect)
apple (AP ple)
tiger (TI ger)

Compare these sounds to the iambs. Can you hear the difference?

A three-syllable foot with the strongest stress first is called a *dactyl*. Here are some one-word examples:

daffodil (DAFF o dill)
elephant (EL e phant)
underwear (UN der wear)

A three-syllable foot with the strongest stress last is an *anapest*. It is not as common as the dactyl. Here are some examples:

underneath (un der NEATH)
interrupt (in ter RUPT)
in the dark (in the DARK)

Rarely, a two-syllable foot such as "head first" can be read with equal stress on both syllables. Such a foot is called a *spondee*.

Metrical Lines

A poem may have from one to eight or more metrical feet per line. A line in a poem is named for the number of feet it contains:

number of feet	name of line
one	monometer
two	dimeter
three	trimeter
four	tetrameter
five	pentameter*
six	hexameter
seven	heptameter
eight	octameter

* A pentameter line is the most common type of line in poetry. It is about the length that most people can comfortably speak.

A line of poetry can be described by both its meter and its length. A line with iambic meter and five feet is called iambic pentameter. It sounds like this: da DUM da DUM da DUM da DUM da DUM. Here are some examples:

I wish I had another purple pen.
She found the key beneath the empty chair.
My dog is white with spots around her eyes.

When you read poetry, pay attention to rhythm and line length. When you write poetry, experiment with different line lengths and meters. See what sounds best for your subject.

Scansion

Scansion is the process of determining the meter of a poem. To see whether your lines have consistent meter, you can scan them. The easiest way to begin is to mark each heavily stressed syllable:

```
 /    /    /    /
Mary had a little lamb.
```

Each metrical foot has one heavily stressed syllable, so as soon as you count heavy stresses, you know how many feet are in a line. This line has four feet, but you can't tell what type they are yet.

Next, mark each lightly stressed syllable:

```
 / ˘  / ˘  / ˘  /
Mary had a little lamb.
```

The line above has four heavily stressed syllables but only three lightly stressed syllables. Are these feet trochees (/˘) or iambs (˘/)? To find out, look at the rest of the stanza:

```
˘   /    ˘    /  ˘    /
Its fleece was white as snow.
˘    / ˘  /    ˘   / ˘  /
And ev'rywhere that Mary went,
˘   /    ˘   /   ˘  /
The lamb was sure to go.
```

Each line except for the first one begins with a lightly stressed syllable followed by a heavily stressed syllable and keeps up that pattern. All the feet in the last three lines are iambic, so that is the main pattern of the stanza.

The next step is to divide the lines into feet:

Notice that lines 2 and 4 have only three feet. They are iambic trimeter. Lines 1 and 3, with four feet each, are iambic tetrameter.

Counting the number of syllables in each line can help you be more exact. The first foot of line 1 has only one syllable, which is perfectly fine. Slight variations within and between lines can make scansion more challenging, but they also make the rhythm more interesting. So don't worry if your meter is not perfect. Just try to be as consistent as possible.

Rhyme

I love the sounds of rhyming words, and I enjoy the challenge of finding the best words that say what I mean and also sound right.

But not everyone feels that way. So it's a good thing that not every poem has to rhyme. You can choose whether to use rhyme, depending on your subject and the way you feel about it. Many good poems do not rhyme.

If you do enjoy the challenge of rhyming, have fun with it! You can get better with practice. Be careful not to let the effort to rhyme lead you off in different directions. Use a rhyming word only if it says exactly what you mean better than another word. One way to make sure you stay on track is to write what you want to say without rhyme first and add rhyme later.

Rhyming dictionaries can be helpful tools, but all their options can lead you astray. Try using a rhyming dictionary for warm-up exercises to start your brain working on sound and rhythm.

Rebecca's poem explores the night in rhyme.

Nighttime

Through the night I wander far,
searching for a fallen star,
searching for a lit up moon,
beckoning night has come too soon.

Rebecca Embar, Grade 4

To illustrate three things that often go wrong when writing in rhyme, I wrote a poem that includes examples of what not to do. Focus on the rhyming words. Can you find all three problems?

Scratchy Cat

Scratchy cat
in the window sat
wearing a hat
looking for rats.

Look at the last word in each line. Can you see that they don't all quite rhyme? *Cat*, *sat*, and *hat* do. But the *s* on the end of *rats* makes it not a perfect rhyme. Word pairs like *hat* and *rats* or *down* and *ground* or *rain* and *paint* are called off rhymes, slant rhymes, or near rhymes. Try to avoid using them if you can find something better. Slant rhymes can make a poem sound as if the poet didn't care enough or try hard enough to find exactly the right words. To fix this issue, we could change the last line to "looking for a rat."

Next, look at line 2. See how the words are arranged in a weird order so the rhyming word lands at the end of the line? "In the window sat" sounds awkward, or forced. "Sat in the window" sounds more natural. But then a new problem pops up: *window* doesn't rhyme with *cat.* One way to solve that problem would be to switch some of the lines around. I did that in the next draft.

Finally, avoid overusing simple rhymes. Rhymes like *cat*, *sat*, and *hat* (and *mat*, *flat*, *gnat*, and so on) are easy and obvious. With too many simple, one-syllable words, a poem becomes predictable, and that can mean boring. Try to include some longer, more exciting words in your rhyming pairs. What if instead of sitting in the window, the cat leaped up there? Then we could call him "acrobat." That sounds more interesting and more fitting than "wearing a hat." See the next chapter for the next draft of "Scratchy Cat."

Rhyme does not belong only at the ends of lines. Rhyme within a line is called *internal rhyme.* Even if you want to avoid the pressure of rhyming in a regular pattern, you might enjoy a little rhyme once in a while. Consider rhyming inside a line just for the fun of it. The next poem uses both end rhyme and internal rhyme.

Yellow

Yellow is like lemonade
Yellow is how fun is made
It sounds like my favorite band
and feels like sand on my feet
Yellow is such a treat.

Gloria Crosbie, Grade 4

Notice that *band* at the end of line 3 rhymes with *sand* in the middle of line 4. Even if you don't want your whole poem to rhyme, you can add interest with a touch of internal rhyme.

Rhyme Schemes

The pattern in a rhyming poem can be described by using a shortcut called a *rhyme scheme.* A rhyme scheme describes the lines that rhyme by assigning a letter to each line in alphabetical order beginning with a. Every line that rhymes is given the same letter as its rhyming partner.

For "Nighttime," the rhyme scheme is aabb: lines 1 and 2 (ending with *far* and *star*) rhyme, and lines 3 and 4 (*moon* and *soon*) rhyme.

For "Mary Had a Little Lamb," the rhyme scheme is abcb: line 1(*lamb*) has no rhyme, lines 2 and 4 (*snow* and *go*) rhyme, and line 3 (*went*) has no rhyme.

For "Yellow," the rhyme scheme is aabcc (*lemonade*, *made*, *band*, *feet*, *treat*).

In many rhyming poems, lines 1 and 3 rhyme, and so do lines 2 and 4. That rhyme scheme is abab.

Try to identify the rhyme schemes of poems you read. As you write, play around with different rhyme schemes.

Repetition

What do you do when you want to remember something? Do you say it to yourself again and again until you learn it? That's using repetition. Repetition is an effective technique in poetry. It helps create a pattern in a poem. It can help us remember. It can add emphasis to a certain word or phrase. It can connect the parts of a poem to each other. Repetition ties Rahel's poem together.

Blowing in the Wind

The tree's branches are
blowing in the wind.
Like a cradle rocking
blowing in the wind.
It sounds like a baby crying
blowing in the wind.
The branches are swiveling
blowing in the wind.
Seems like a Mom saying,
"Shhhh!"
blowing in the wind.

Rahel Spilka, Grade 2

Abigail's poem also makes a point with repetition.

Sleep

Sleep, sleep, sleep
You fall asleep
so fast and sound
sleep, sleep, sleep
You dream
as sweetly as a rose
at spring
But you snore
as loud as an elephant's big feet
zzzzzzzzzz
sleep, sleep, sleep
the gross taste in your mouth
is like a dirty sock
being shoved down your throat
Plah!
Finally!
Your mom yells, "Time to get up!"
"Uhhhh. . . O.K.!"
Sleep, sleep, sleep

Abigail Amidzich, Grade 3

Although the tone of this poem changes from beginning to middle to end, the repeating line "sleep, sleep, sleep" ties it together.

Writing Time

Now look at the images and exciting words you have listed so far. Consider introducing or reinforcing one or more of the patterns described in this chapter: rhythm, rhyme, and repetition.

To hear the rhythm, read your poem aloud. Does it sound the way you want it to sound? Look for opportunities to improve the rhythm by substituting more effective words, rephrasing lines, and adding or deleting.

Are you using rhyme? Try some simple rhyme schemes at first, and then expand your options. Remember that a poem does not need to rhyme and that even a little rhyme can add flavor. If you set up a strict rhyming pattern, readers will expect it to continue throughout a poem. But if you want to use a few rhyming words at strategic points, consider a sprinkling of internal rhyme.

If your poem includes a word, a phrase, a line, or even a stanza that you want to use more than once, go ahead. Just make sure that what you repeat is important to the poem, or it can feel or sound overdone. In my clustering poem about the stone on the beach, I decided to repeat the word *stone* in two strategic spots.

Before you go on to the last step, look over your work again. Does your poem sound more like a story? Cross out any unnecessary words. In poetry, a fragment can be stronger than a sentence.

Experiment with different arrangements. Play with the order until it feels and sounds right. You might want to combine two lines into one or break up one line into two. You might need to add a transition to make a smooth connection from one line to the next.

In my stone poem, something seemed to be missing between "tumbled by waves" and "I hold this oval pebble in my pocket." Before I could pick up the stone, I had to find it on the beach. So I added a line to fill the gap. Here is the poem so far:

gray as a storm cloud
rough as a bumpy road
stone
tumbled by waves
tossed to the beach
stone
I hold this oval pebble in my pocket
and remember stillness

Your poem-in-progress needs one more important step to make it look like a poem. The next chapter discusses form.

Step 5. Creating the Form

In most stories (and in books like this one), the words in each line stretch from one margin all the way across to the other. Sentences are combined into paragraphs. The first line of a paragraph might be indented, but most lines of text begin at the left margin and continue across from there.

In a poem, the lines do not have to reach across a whole page. They can be short or long, similar or different. You can left justify, center, or right justify lines in a poem or tab them into different positions. You can group them together in stanzas. You determine what shape your poem takes on the page when you decide on the length and position of each line.

Line Breaks

You might have divided your poem into lines as you wrote it. If you haven't, this step will help you decide where to end each line. If you have, read this chapter to understand some reasons for line breaks and consider other options.

The most common place to break a line is at the end of a complete thought. In my stone poem in the previous chapter, every line expresses a separate thought.

In Christopher's poem as well, each line includes one thought.

Turtle

I am a turtle
slow as a slug.
I am plump as a pumpkin.
I can swim as fast as the wind
using my strong leathery legs.

Christopher Haasler, Grade 3

Breaking a line at the end of a thought can cause a reader to stop at that spot and think.

Breaking a line in the middle of a thought and pushing a word or phrase to the next line is called *enjambment*. It can make a reader want to rush ahead to see what happens next.

In Christine's poem, notice how line breaks in the middle of thoughts make you hurry up and read faster.

Arizona

the sand there
is as yellow as a banana

a cactus
is as green as a Granny Smith apple

the sand makes
the soles of your feet
steam

the sun's
beaming rays
beat down
and warm you
like a hot day at the
beach

Christine McLinn, Grade 4

Line breaks can help create a shape on the page. Compare the loose double diamond structure of "Arizona" to the triangular "Turtle" and the squarish shape of my stone poem. The length and placement of every line create a poem's shape.

Short lines grab the reader. They can make a poem feel excited or rushed. Long lines can meander around and take their sweet time getting to the point. They can make a poem feel more thoughtful or deliberate.

Lines of similar lengths can reinforce a regular rhythm. A change in line length can affect the pace of a poem by causing a reader to speed up or slow down.

Words can receive more attention because of their placement, so you can break a line at a specific spot if you want to emphasize certain words. Usually, the last word in a line receives the most attention, and the first word receives the second-most attention.

In Jimmy's poem, notice the emphasis on the first and last word in each line.

Bald Eagle

Bald eagle
Shimmering
In the sun
Head white as paper,
Body brown as dead grass,
Racing light,
To a fish,
Its talons,
Eight iridescent razors,
Sure omen of death,
Diving,
Its muscles contract,
Speeding needle,
Zooming to the ground,
It swoops,
The whoosh of air,
A glittering, sharp sword blade,
Cutting through the silent night,
Bald eagle!

Jimmy Macken, Grade 6

Sometimes a line break simply feels right. Even if you can't explain why, you might know where a line should end. Trust your judgment.

Stanzas

Lines in a poem can be grouped into stanzas just as sentences in a story form paragraphs. The white space between stanzas creates an even longer break than a line break. That space can give the reader a chance to stop and think. Many rhyming poems include several stanzas that all follow the same pattern or rhyme scheme.

Emily's poem shows her thoughts about oak trees.

Praise to the Oak Tree

Praise to the oak tree
Standing tall and still
On the grassy slopes
Of the forest hill.

Praise to the oak tree
Leaves flying in the breeze
Oak tree, dearest one
The pride of all strong trees.

Sorry, conifers—
Maples, palm, birch.
Prideful oak tree—
You let the birds perch.

Praise to the oak tree
Tall, brave, true
Dearest lively oak
Standing in the sky of blue.

The wind may scream
Wisp, whisper, howl
But dearest elder oak—
You house the majestic owl.

And in the dark of night
Shadows lurk under you
I may come visit
under the light of the silver moon
Tall, gnarled branches stretching in the sky
Brave, wise, a tree that's true.

Emily Lentz, Grade 5

If your poem calls for thoughtful consideration or attention to several concepts, think about breaking it up into stanzas.

Writing Time

When you read a poem, you often pause briefly at the end of a line. To add line breaks, read your poem aloud and listen for those pauses. Wherever your voice stops, draw a vertical mark between the words. Those places are the most obvious places to break the lines. Copy your poem over, starting a new line after each vertical mark. You will have a complete draft of your new poem.

Suppose I wrote the next draft of "Scratchy Cat" from Step 4 without breaking the lines. It might look like this.

Scratchy Cat
Scratchy cat, looking for a rat, leaps to the window. Acrobat!

When I read it aloud, my voice naturally stops after the words *cat*, *rat*, and *window*. So I draw a vertical mark at each of those spots.

Scratchy Cat
Scratchy cat, | looking for a rat, | leaps to the window. | Acrobat!

Then I copy the poem over, using those vertical marks to tell me where the line breaks belong.

Scratchy Cat

Scratchy cat,
looking for a rat,
leaps to the window.
Acrobat!

Now do the same with your poem: read it aloud, mark the spots where you pause, and copy the poem over with a line break where you marked each pause.

Reread it with those line breaks. Does it look the way you want it to look? Does it sound the way you want it to sound? Does it need to be broken up into more than one stanza? Experiment with different variations until you are satisfied that your poem looks and sounds best.

Titles

Have you given your poem a title? Not every poem needs a title, but when you finish a draft, it's a good time to consider the possibilities. A title can tell what the poem is about. It can be a key word or phrase from the poem, like "Scratchy Cat." I decided to give my poem about the stone I found on the beach the simple title "Found."

The title could be the first or last part of the poem you write. It might be the idea that sparks the whole poem. Or it might not come to you until long after the poem is finished.

After you finish this step, you'll have a complete draft of a poem. Hooray for you! You can either keep working on your poem or put it aside to look at again later. Poems are almost never finished in one draft, so be prepared to take another look. The second-last chapter gives you some help with revising.

Forms

Poets have been writing and reciting poems for so long that many traditional forms of poetry have developed over the years. Some have definite rhyme schemes, some have specific rhythms, some have a certain number of syllables in each line. A huge variety of options is available, from acrostic to sonnet, cinquain to villanelle.

Many poets find a kind of freedom when writing within the structure of a form. Because the patterns are already defined, all the poet has to do is supply the best words in the proper order. A strict form can actually free you to write about a difficult subject.

Entire books are devoted to describing and giving examples of poetic forms. If you'd like to explore some options, look for a reference book such as *The Book of Forms: A Handbook of Poetics* by Lewis Turco. Here are some forms you might enjoy.

Free Verse

The term *free verse* can be confusing because the form is not completely free of patterns. A free verse poem does not have a regular rhyme scheme. The lines can be of any length, and they do not have to be the same length. Although the form has no regular defined rhythm, a free verse poem still can have rhythm. If you've followed this book step by step and decided to write without using rhyme, you probably have just written a free verse poem.

See the following books for examples.

River Friendly, River Wild by Jane Kurtz

All the Small Poems and Fourteen More by Valerie Worth

Haiku

Haiku is a form that originated in Japan hundreds of years ago. Because haiku are brief and spare, writing them helps you appreciate how much every word counts in a poem. When you write haiku, try to avoid using *and*, *the*, and any other words that add length but not substance.

The traditional haiku form has seventeen syllables in three lines. The first line has five, the second has seven, and the third has five. But haiku originally focused on sound rather than syllables, so many poets do not count syllables. Haiku translated from another language can also differ from the traditional form because the translator focused on the meaning rather than the syllable count. Haiku can have more or fewer than seventeen syllables and one, two, three, four, or even five lines. Keep them short and simple.

Haiku are poems about everyday things. They focus on a single moment or experience, usually involving nature. Haiku should refer to a season, so include a seasonal word or mention the weather or a plant or animal that symbolizes a certain time of year. Haiku are written in the present tense, so if you write about an event, write about it as if it is happening right now.

Haiku usually include either one concrete image or two images that contrast or complement each other. Many haiku contain a surprise or turning point between two lines.

Onomatopoeia and alliteration appear in haiku, but haiku rarely use titles, prepositions, similes, metaphors, or complete sentences.

See the following books for examples.

Won-Ton: A Cat Tale Told in Haiku by Lee Wardlaw

Guyku: A Year of Haiku for Boys by Bob Raczka

Black Swan/White Crow by J. Patrick Lewis

Wing Nuts: Screwy Haiku by Paul B. Janeczko and J. Patrick Lewis

If Not for the Cat: Haiku by Jack Prelutsky

Haiku: Asian Arts and Crafts for Creative Kids by Patricia Donegan

Stone Bench in an Empty Park edited by Paul B. Janeczko

Cricket Never Does: A Collection of Haiku and Tanka by Myra Cohn Livingston

Limericks

The limerick form probably started in Ireland. All limericks have five lines, and most are humorous. Lines one, two, and five have three feet, and they rhyme. Lines three and four have two feet, and they rhyme. Most feet are anapests. To get a feel for the rhythm, read lots of limericks aloud.

The first line of a typical limerick refers to a character and a location; for example, "There once was a girl from Green Bay." The second line describes a quality, an activity, or something else about the character. The next two lines lead up to the last one, which might be a punch line, a clever twist, or a surprise ending.

For examples of limericks, see *Grimericks* by Susan Pearson.

Odes

An ode is a poem that speaks directly to a person or thing. An ode can praise a person, celebrate an occasion, or describe the natural world. Odes were originally meant to be sung.

Several strict ode forms include specific rhythm patterns and structures. An ode can also have an irregular or loose structure or rely on a structure the poet defines.

For examples of odes, see *Neighborhood Odes* by Gary Soto.

List Poems

List poems are also called catalog poems or inventory poems. The structure resembles a list and usually relies on repetition. In many list poems, several lines begin with the same words. Abby's list poem describes her dog.

Brie

She reminds me of the wind
          whish
She is smooth yet rough
She is fast like the wind
She runs with the deer
          zoom
She smells like sweat
She has eyes like an
          owl
She has vision like a hawk
She is my dog
She is my pride
She is Brie

Abby Justus, Grade 5

For more examples of list poems, see *Falling Down the Page: A Book of List Poems*, edited by Georgia Heard.

Shape Poems

Shape poems are poems whose words form a shape, usually of the subject of the poem. They are also called concrete poems or spatial poems. Poems about simple objects fit most easily into shapes.

The words of a shape poem must make sense with or without the shape. To make sure you put the emphasis on the meaning of the poem rather than its shape, write the poem first. Then you can draw it in an appropriate shape.

In Billy's poem, the words form an outline of the shape.

Fish

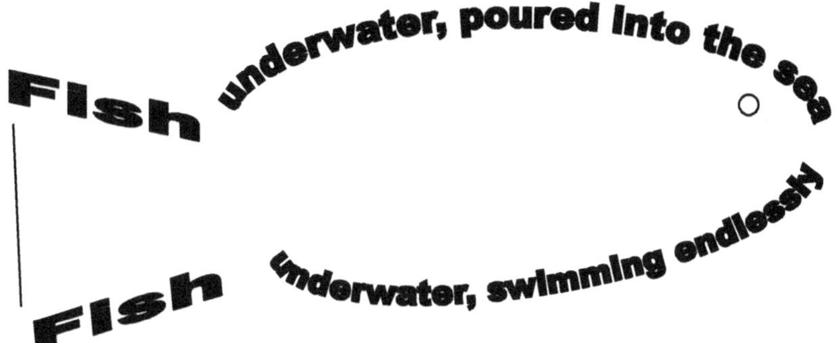

Billy Macken, Grade 2

In my poem, the words fill in the shape.

Stapler

Alligator hears a rustle,
Lies in wait with gaping jaws,
Silver glinting in the shadows.
Chomp! Leaves its tooth marks.

In Microsoft® Office Word, you can form text into shapes with WordArt.

See the following books for more shape poem examples.

Splish Splash and *Flicker Flash: Poems* by Joan Bransfield Graham

Technically, It's Not My Fault: Concrete Poems and *Blue Lipstick: Concrete Poems* by John Grandits

A Poke in the I, edited by Paul B. Janeczko

Doodle Dandies: Poems that Take Shape by J. Patrick Lewis

Come to My Party and Other Shape Poems by Heidi Bee Roemer

More Reading Suggestions

In a library or bookstore, you'll probably find poetry books in a separate poetry section. They are usually in alphabetical order by the poet's last name.

If you find a poetry collection you enjoy, look for more titles by the same poet. When you read anthologies that include many poets' work, notice the names of the poets whose writing you like. Then look for more of their poems.

So many wonderful poetry collections are available that I can't possibly list them all here. For a long and growing list of my favorites, see my web site, www.joannmacken.com.

Books About Writing Poetry

Here are some other books about writing poetry that might help you with your process and your poems. I hope these suggestions are helpful to you. Happy writing!

Ralph Fletcher: *Poetry Matters: Writing a Poem from the Inside Out*
Paul B. Janeczko: *Poetry from A to Z: A Guide for Young Writers*
How to Write Poetry
Seeing the Blue Between: Advice and Inspiration for Young Poets
A Kick in the Head: An Everyday Guide to Poetic Forms
Myra Cohn Livingston: *Poem-Making: Ways to Begin Writing Poetry*
Jack Prelutsky: *Pizza, Pigs, and Poetry: How to Write a Poem*
Margaret Ryan: *Extraordinary Poetry Writing*
Laura Purdie Salas: *Write Your Own Poetry*
Allan Wolf: *Immersed in Verse*

Writing Exercises

You can use these writing exercises to loosen up, warm up, or generate new ideas.

Working on Ideas

Pick a word, a topic, or an idea at random and see how you can make it your own. If you have a writing partner or writing group, try choosing one idea you can all write about and see how many different approaches you can find to the same suggestion.

You could even pick a theme and write several poems about it. See the following collections for examples.

Button Up! Wrinkled Rhymes by Alice Schertle
Dark Emperor and Other Poems of the Night by Joyce Sidman
Emma Dilemma: Big Sister Poems by Kristine O'Connell George
Here's a Little Poem: A Very First Book of Poetry collected by Jane Yolen and Andrew Fusek Peters
I Am the Book: Poems selected by Lee Bennett Hopkins
Insectlopedia by Douglas Florian
Mirror, Mirror: A Book of Reversible Verse by Marilyn Singer
Night Garden: Poems from the World of Dreams by Janet S. Wong
Over in the Pink House: New Jump Rope Rhymes by Rebecca Kai Dotlich
Today at the Bluebird Café: A Branchful of Birds by Deborah Ruddell
The Tree That Time Built: A Celebration of Nature, Science and Imagination selected by Mary Ann Hoberman and Linda Winston

Working on Imagery

Choose two objects and see what characteristics you can find that they have in common. How is a table like a horse? How is an egg like a marble? How is a planet like a coin? Use that image to write a draft of a new poem.

Working on Connections

I call this exercise "String of Pearls" because it forms a chain of connected thoughts. Start by writing "String of Pearls" or any other word or phrase you choose. Keep writing whatever comes into your head, and write without stopping. Each entry must relate somehow to the one that came before. You can make a new connection by rhyming, by changing a word or part of a word, by starting a new phrase with the end of the previous one, or by any other method that pops into your mind.

Working on Wordplay

Make a list of words you like, whether you are attracted to the sound or the meaning. Keep your list in a notebook or journal. Then look for opportunities to use the words. Some of my favorites are *silver*, *kerfuffle*, *wedge*, *mellifluous*, *periwinkle*, and *mulligatawny*.

Working on Rhythm

Think of a song or a nursery rhyme with a regular beat. Then make up new words that fit the rhythm.

Working on Rhyme

Use a rhyming dictionary. Choose several words that rhyme and try to write a poem around them. Make sure your poem makes sense! (Hint: Try a limerick. The humorous form works well with words that seem unrelated at first.)

Working on Form

Find a poem you like and imitate its form. Write about a similar topic or something completely different. Keep the meter and line length the same as your example poem.

Revising

You've worked hard to write your poem, so why should you revise it? To make it even better! Revision can make your poem more specific, more vivid, more humorous, more serious, more like what you meant to say. Few first drafts are so good that they have no room for improvement. Most poets revise again and again until their poems sparkle and every single word is exactly right.

Revising a poem can be like solving a puzzle. Add exciting words and cut out more ordinary ones. Rearrange the lines and words to improve the rhythm, sound, and clarity.

Even if you write your first drafts on paper, you might find it easier to revise on a computer. You can move words, lines, or whole stanzas around and move them back if you decide you like the original version better. You can even save several versions of a poem and take your time thinking about which you prefer.

Condensing

Most stories contain complete sentences. A poem might not. A poem can consist entirely of fragments or phrases. In fact, a poem can be more interesting, stronger, and more focused if it does not include complete sentences. Remember that the fewer words you use, the more direct and powerful your poems can be. Try to use one strong word instead of two or more that mean the same thing. In a poem, every word counts.

Much of revising is cutting out unnecessary words. Delete or cross out any words you don't absolutely need to make your point. Try to cut out adjectives and adverbs, especially words such as *very* that add length but not meaning. Choose strong language that doesn't need modifiers.

Tense

Look over the verbs in your poem. Are they all in the same tense, or do they switch back and forth from past to present to future and back again? (For example, "I jump" is present tense—it is happening right now. "I jumped" is past tense—it already happened. "I will jump" means it will happen in the future.) Try to keep the tense consistent.

Point of View

From whose point of view does your poem speak? Your own? That is first person. (I jump.) If you are speaking directly to someone or something, you are using second person. (You jump.) If you are speaking about someone or something, that's third person. (He jumps. She jumps. They jump.) Unless you are purposely writing from two or more points of view, try to keep the point of view in your poem consistent.

Back to the Beginning

One good way to revise a poem is to go back through the same five steps you used to create it.

1. Idea. Does the poem say what you intended? If not, what could you change to make it say what you mean?
2. Imagery. Do your images paint a clear picture? Do they reinforce each other? Can you think of any others?
3. Language. Do you see any ordinary words you could replace with something more exciting or original? Read the poem aloud and listen to the sounds of the words. Do they fit the subject?
4. Patterns: rhythm, rhyme, and repetition. Listen again. Is the rhythm regular or choppy? Does the poem flow at a pace that fits its subject? If you've used rhyming words, do they rhyme exactly and also express what you mean? Have you used repetition effectively? Would it help if you did?

5. Form. Check the line breaks. Does the poem look the way it should on the page? When you read the poem, does your voice pause in the right places?

Remember that not every poem includes all the techniques described in this book. If you've tried a certain technique, look and listen to see whether it's effective. If you haven't tried one, consider whether it would improve your poem. Has your revision accomplished what you intended? If not, try again!

Mechanics

Before you declare your poem complete, check the spelling, grammar, and punctuation. If they are all correct and understandable, your poem will be clearer to readers.

If you work on a computer, you can use its spell-checking software. Just be careful not to rely on it to distinguish between different words that are spelled correctly. You can also use a dictionary or thesaurus. Ask a teacher, friend, or parent to look over your work if you need help. Be sure to compare the revision to the original to make sure no words were lost or changed accidentally.

You do not have to capitalize words in a poem as you would in a story. Some poets capitalize the first word in each line. Some poets capitalize words that begin new thoughts just as they would the first words in new sentences. Some poets do not capitalize any words at all. Do what feels right for each poem while keeping the reader in mind.

Punctuation in a poem is not necessarily standard, either. If your poem contains complete sentences, you can punctuate them as if they were in a story. If you prefer, you can omit punctuation. Line breaks and stanza breaks might create enough pauses for readers. Just be sure they can understand your meaning.

Critique Groups

When you are ready, consider sharing your poems with others who can help you improve. Constructive criticism can help you make your work stronger. Try to find a group of like-minded writers you trust to read your poems. You might want to meet on a regular basis, either in person or by e-mail.

But don't rush to share. Wait until your work is really ready. Then choose people who can be tactful and not hurt your feelings even when they have to tell you that something still needs work. Be willing to assume that they might be correct, even if only for the time it takes to try what they suggest. Listen carefully and focus on the comments, not on the person who made them. Even if you don't agree, notice any parts of your poems that other readers don't understand. Then work on those spots.

Be a good critiquing partner, too. When you read others' work, look for the positive and mention it first. Be tactful as well as honest. If you're not sure about a meaning, ask a question: Is this what you intended? Don't assume that every poem is about the writer's own experience; it could be imagined or based on someone else's life. Phrase your comments the way you would want to hear them if you were in the other poet's place.

How to Know When a Poem Is Finished

Don't worry about how many drafts it takes to finish a poem. The important thing is that you are happy with the result. Some poems need only a little tinkering or tweaking; others require many major revisions. Keep working until you are satisfied. Then put your poem aside for a while so you can take a fresh look at it later. If you are still happy with it then, consider it done. If not, try again.

How do you know when a poem is finished? Answer this question: Are your revisions changing it for the better it or just changing it? When you no longer see actual improvement or room for it, call the poem finished. Then celebrate!

Publishing Your Work

When you are satisfied that your poem says what you want to say in the best possible way, you might want to show it to others. (You might want to keep some poems to yourself, which is also fine.) A poem can make a wonderful gift for a friend or family member. You can write a poem to mark a special occasion or to say something special. What could be more personal?

Self-Publishing

If you have access to a computer with word-processing software, you can format your poem and print it. If you write a poem in a class, you and your classmates could print the whole class's poems and bind them together into a book. You can even illustrate them and make copies. Then you can share them with your families and other classes.

Publishing in School

Does your school have a newspaper, newsletter, magazine, or yearbook? Consider submitting your poetry. If your school has no publication, why not start one? Recruit other interested poets and ask a teacher for help.

Publishing Resources

If you want to publish a poem where many people can read it, consider submitting it to a magazine, anthology, or web site.

The annual market guide *Children's Writer's and Illustrator's Market* lists magazines and anthologies that publish the work of young writers in a section called "Young Writer's and Illustrator's Markets." Many libraries carry this book and others like it.

The Teaching Authors group blog includes a list of markets for young writers at TeachingAuthors.com.

Good luck! Have fun! Keep writing!

About JoAnn Early Macken

Photo: Gene Macken

JoAnn Early Macken is the author of five picture books:

- *Baby Says "Moo!"* (Disney-Hyperion, 2011)
- *Waiting Out the Storm* (Candlewick Press, 2010)
- *Flip, Float, Fly: Seeds on the Move* (Holiday House, 2008)
- *Sing-Along Song* (Viking, 2004)
- *Cats on Judy* (Whispering Coyote Press, 1997)

JoAnn's poems have been published in several children's magazines and anthologies, and she has also written more than one hundred nonfiction books for educational publishers.

JoAnn earned her M.F.A. in Writing for Children and Young Adults from Vermont College of Fine Arts. She teaches writing at three Wisconsin colleges, and she speaks about poetry and writing to children and adults at schools, libraries, and conferences.

JoAnn reads and writes in Wisconsin, where she also gardens, takes photographs, walks the family dog, and paddles a canoe whenever she can. Visit her web site at www.joannmacken.com or send her a message at JoAnn@joannmacken.com.

Acknowledgments

Many people have helped me with this book and the process that inspired it. I especially appreciate the teachers who welcomed me into their classrooms and the students who wrote poems and contributed suggestions.

My writing group (Ann Angel, Dori Chaconas, Gretchen Will Mayo, Lisa Moser, and Sharon Addy) read draft after draft of this manuscript (and others) and offered helpful suggestions. My Vermont College advisors (Ellen Howard, Norma Fox Mazer, Phyllis Root, and Amy Ehrlich) and classmates (The Hive: Gretchen from my writing group plus Carolyn Crimi, Jeanne Marie Grunwell Ford, Phyllis Harris, Lindan Johnson, Laura Kemp, Carolyn Marsden, Carmela Martino, Mary Ann Rodman, April Pulley Sayre, Meribeth Shank, and Gretchen Woelfle), my former TeachingAuthors.com blogmates (Carmela, Jeanne Marie, and Mary Ann from the Hive plus April Halprin Wayland and Esther Hershenhorn), my mother (Mary Early), and my sisters (Peggy Krzyzewski, Judy Sheldon, Sarah Tugan, Eileen Early, Bridget Mulgrew, and P.J. Early) provided support in countless ways. They all deserve my deep and unlimited gratitude.

My family (Gene, Jimmy, and Billy Macken) put up with my tunnel vision, alternately held my hand and stayed out of my way, read, listened, cooked, cleaned, and let me stay up late when I needed to keep going and sleep in when I needed to rest. Thanks, guys! I couldn't have imagined this without you.

Index

Poems

A

B

C

D

E

F

G

H

I

J

L

M

N

O

P

R

S

T

V

W

www.ingramcontent.com/pod-product-compliance
Lightning Source LLC
Chambersburg PA
CBHW060041040426
42331CB00032B/1996

* 9 7 8 0 9 8 5 7 6 5 0 0 2 *